Short Meditations on Psalm 119

by

Fletcher Matandika

Dedication

This book is dedicated to my father, Rev. R. A. Matandika. Thank you, Dad, for teaching me to love the Word of God through your own example. May the LORD continue to bless you and use you greatly in His vineyard. I love you!

Table of Contents

Table of Contents

Preface

This little book is meant to kindle your interest in the Word of God in general and in Psalm 119 in particular. To go through this psalm is to literally put yourself in the path of God's grace. While this is true of the entire Word of God, it is especially true of Psalm 119. As it is commonly said, all of Scripture is inspired by God (i.e. it is His Word), but all Scripture is not equally inspiring. To illustrate, you will find that reading the first chapter of 1 Chronicles is quite a different experience from that of reading Psalm 1, Psalm 19 or Psalm 119. You get the point.

The material in this book is intended for prayerful devotional study. It has been arranged in such a way as to stir your soul and stimulate you to regularly meditate on the Word of God for your soul's nourishment. Deuteronomy 8:3 tells us that "…man lives by every word that comes from the mouth of God." God has promised to nourish and sustain the souls of His people through His Word among other things. As you put yourself in the path of His grace, He will see to it that you have your fill.

My only plea with you, dear reader, is that you will be a good Berean (Acts 17:11). Check everything written in this book and make sure that it is in agreement with the Word of God. Should you find any conflict between the material presented in this book and the clear teaching of Scripture, then I beg you, by all means, please discard this book and hold on to the faithful, reliable and inspired teaching of the Holy Scriptures which alone can make you wise for salvation through faith in Christ Jesus (2 Timothy 3:15).

May the Lord use this book to save sinners and sanctify the saints to the praise, glory and honor of His Holy Name.

Through Jesus Christ,

Fletcher Matandika

Introduction

Psalm 119 happens to be the longest chapter in the whole Bible. It is rich, deep and wide in its scope. As is the case with the whole book of Psalms, Psalm 119 alone covers a wide range of human experiences and emotions. It is intended to drive the reader deeper into the Word of God.

This psalm is organized using the 22 letters of the Hebrew alphabet. Thus, it has 22 sections in total. Each section contains eight verses. That is how we end up with the 176 verses that make this great psalm.

The main theme of this wonderful chapter is the God's Word. Masterfully arranged, it draws us in and takes us to the Fountain of Living Water so that we may drink from it to our soul's nourishment and satisfaction.

Psalm 119 is like a deep well which never runs dry. The more you drink from it, the more there is to drink. As you drink from this well, you will surely find yourself overflowing with much joy and happiness in the Word of

God and in the God of the Word. Indeed, you will find yourself saying with the Psalmist, "O how I love Your law! It is my meditation all the day;" (Psalm 119:97) and "How sweet are Your Words to my taste, sweeter than honey to my mouth" (Psalm 119:103).

One great benefit that you will most certainly enjoy from studying and meditating on Psalm 119 is that you will be able to pray better. This psalm contains short phrases and sentences that are quite memorable and easy to repeat in prayer. The words are rich with meaning, soul stirring, expressing our deepest longings before the LORD our God in His own language. It doesn't' get better than that. Your praying will definitely improve as you master this psalm and as you are mastered by it. I challenge you; your prayers will never be the same.

Finally, you will see Christ written all over this psalm from the beginning to the end. That is the best part. I have tried to make the connections between what the psalmist is saying in this psalm and the Person of Jesus Christ who is the Central Theme of all the Scriptures. It is marvellously refreshing to see how each section of this great psalm finds its ultimate meaning and fulfillment in Christ Jesus.

Two things will remain the focus of my prayers for you as you meditate on each section of this grand psalm: Firstly, I pray that you will grow more in love with Christ and His Word and find in Him all the depth of the riches and the wisdom and knowledge of God. Secondly, I pray that as you grow more in love with Jesus Christ and His Word, you may also grow in grace – becoming more like Him with every passing day.

I am very glad and grateful that in the providence of God, you have gotten a hold of this little book. May the LORD use it to bless you and deepen your love for Him and His Word as only He can. May you discover afresh through Psalm 119, that Faithful Friend Who sticks closer than a brother, the Lord Jesus Christ, our Savior even as you are transformed into His likeness day by day.

Your friend and brother in Christ,

Fletcher Matandika

True Blessedness
(Psalm 119:1-8, *Aleph*)

Blessed are those whose way is blameless, who walk in the law of the LORD! Blessed are those who keep His testimonies, who seek Him with their whole heart, who also do no wrong, but walk in His ways! You have commanded Your precepts to be kept diligently. Oh, that my ways may be steadfast in keeping Your statutes! Then I shall not be put to shame, having my eyes fixed on all Your commandments. I will keep Your statutes, do not utterly forsake me.

Psalm 1 equates blessedness with walking in God's law. Psalm 32 talks of blessedness in terms of God offering the forgiveness of sin to the sinner once and for all. Here, the psalmist brings these two great truths together and shows us that blamelessness before God is true blessedness. This man's blessedness is not found in himself. Rather, it is found in the mercy of God towards undeserving sinners like you and me. The psalmist has in mind, a man of God, a believer, one who lives his life under the influence of the Lord Jesus Christ and His Holy Spirit. He is happy in the Lord. He delights in His Word and shuns all evil. Therefore, he longs for more of God's Word in order that he may praise Him with an upright heart. Through His Word, the LORD God offers forgiveness for sin to all who trust in Jesus Christ and seek to walk in His ways under the power and influence of the Holy Spirit.

LORD, thank you for the blessing of forgiveness which has been made available to me through Christ Jesus and His cross.

"My sin, O the bliss of this glorious thought;
my sin not in part but the whole;
is nailed to the cross and I bear it no more…"

Teach me Your righteous rules that I may praise You with an upright heart through Jesus Christ. Amen!

The Divine Cure for Sin
(Psalm 119:9-19, *Beth*)

How can a young man keep his way pure? By guarding it according to Your Word. With my whole heart I seek You; let me not wander from Your commandments! I have stored up Your Word in my heart, that I might not sin against You. Blessed are You, O LORD; teach me Your statutes! With my lips I declare all the rules of Your mouth. In the way of Your testimonies I delight as much as in all riches. I will meditate on Your precepts and fix my eyes on Your ways. I will delight in Your statutes; I will not forget Your Word.

On his seventeenth birthday, John Piper, founder and teacher at Desiring God Ministries, received a precious Book from his parents with the following inscription: "Son, this Book will keep you from sin and sin will keep you from this Book." The "Book" in reference here was the Bible. What a precious gift we have been given from the LORD God Himself to help us in fighting against sin in our lives. The Bible is clear, "All have sinned and fallen short of the glory of God" (Rom. 2:23). We all struggle with sin. God's Word is the divine cure for sin through the blood of Jesus Christ, our Savior. God's riches are given to us in Christ through His Word so that we may be rid of all sin (i.e. the sin that we inherited from Adam as well as our own actual sins). In this, we see that God's wisdom is so far above man's wisdom. We therefore need to embrace this precious gift of His Word by laying hold of the Lord Jesus Christ (the Living Word) by faith as He is freely offered to us in the gospel. May He make us holy even as He is holy.

Oh, the depth of the riches
And wisdom and knowledge of God!
How unsearchable are His judgments
And how inscrutable His ways!
"For who has known the mind of the Lord,
Or who has been His counselor?"
"Or who has given a gift to Him
That he might be repaid?"
For from Him and through Him
And to Him are all things.
To Him be glory forever.
Amen
Romans 11:33-36

Open the Eyes of My Heart LORD
(Psalm 119:17-24, *Gimel*)

Deal bountifully with Your servant, that I may live and keep Your Word. Open my eyes, that I may behold wondrous things out of Your law. I am a sojourner on the earth; hide not Your commandments from me! My soul is consumed with longing for Your rules at all times. You rebuke the insolent, accursed ones, who wander from Your commandments. Take away from me scorn and contempt, for I have kept your testimonies. Even though princes sit plotting against me, Your servant will meditate on Your statues. Your testimonies are my delight; they are my counselors.

1 Cor. 2:14 says, "The natural person does not accept the things of the Spirit of God, for they are folly to him, and he is not able to understand them because they are spiritually discerned." Aware of this fact, the psalmist here prays for divine illumination that he may understand God's Word and profit from it (vs. 18). Implied in this prayer is a deep, vibrant and fiery desire for God's truth as revealed in His Word. He says to the LORD, "My soul is *consumed* with longing for Your rules at all times" (vs. 20, emphasis

added). He abandons his pride and gets to the heart of the matter by confessing, "I need You LORD!" In turn, he finds comfort as God's Word is opened up to him. The LORD stands ready to help us understand His Word by His Spirit. We only need to ask. He delights in answering such prayers. As His Spirit opens up the Word to us, we will get a deeper knowledge of Who He is and what He requires of us through Jesus Christ, the Incarnate Word.

Open my eyes, that I may behold wondrous things out of Your law, Amen!

An Enlarged Heart
(Psalm 119:25-32, *Daleth*)

My soul clings to the dust; give me life according to Your Word! When I told of my ways, You answered me; teach me Your statutes! Make me understand the way of Your precepts, and I will meditate on Your wondrous works. My soul melts away for sorrow; strengthen me according to Your Word! Put false ways far from me and graciously teach me Your law! I have chosen the way of faithfulness; I set Your rules before me. I cling to Your testimonies, O LORD; let me not be put to shame! I will run in the way of Your commandments when You enlarge my heart!

Medically, an enlarged heart is terrible news! It spells death! However, spiritually, an enlarged heart is desirable (or at least it should be). In this section, the psalmist welcomes an enlarged heart with great delight! Why? Because spiritually, an enlarged heart spells life. Yes, life in Jesus' Name! Hence the psalmist's prayer at the beginning of this section, "Give me life according to Your Word." In this prayer, the psalmist understands a few things. Firstly, that life is a gift from God. Secondly, that this life has been promised in God's Word.

Thirdly, that if we ask God in faith to give us this life, He will certainly grant it to us. But there is a problem. Our hearts are too small to contain this gift. Sin shrinks our hearts and leaves no room for God and His Word. But praise God that Christ comes and cleanses us of all sin by His blood and thus, our hearts are enlarged (i.e. given the capacity to receive and enjoy the blessing of life in His Name). New life is given to us and we begin to "run" in the way of His commandments. Glory be to His Holy Name.

Enlarge my heart, O LORD that I may walk in Your ways.
Amen!

Divine Word, Divine Teacher
(Psalm 119:33-40, *He*)

Teach me, O LORD, the way of Your statutes; and I will keep it to the end. Give me understanding, that I may keep Your law and observe it with my whole heart. Lead me in the path of Your commandments, for I delight in it. Incline my heart to Your testimonies, and not to selfish gain! Turn my eyes from looking at worthless things; and give me life in Your ways. Confirm to Your servant Your promise, that You may be feared. Turn away the reproach that I dread, for Your rules are good. Behold, I long for Your precepts; in Your righteousness give me life!

"Teach me, O LORD, the way of Your statutes and I will keep it to the end" (v. 33). There is no other way for any man to learn God's Word. We all must be taught God's Word by the Divine Teacher, the Holy Spirit. Christ said to His disciples in John 14:26, "But the Helper, the Holy Spirit, Whom the Father will send in My Name, He will teach you all things and bring to your remembrance all that I have said to you." The Holy Spirit does not only teach us. He also helps us to remember God's Word that we may turn our eyes away from the things of this world to the things of God above. He reminds us that we are pilgrims on the journey to the Celestial City. He warns us, "Do not love the world or the things of the world. If anyone loves the world, the love of the Father is not in him. For all that is in the world – the desires of the flesh and the desires of the eyes and pride of life – is not from the Father but is from the world. And the world is passing away along with its desires, but whoever does the will of God abides forever" (1 John 2:15-17). The psalmist's prayer here is for the preservation of his soul from spiritual danger. He knows that any victory over evil in his life must come from the LORD. Thank God that in Christ, He preserves His own to the end!

Incline my heart to Your testimonies, and not to selfish gain,
Amen!

A Sure Foundation
(Psalm 119:41-48, *Vav*)

Let Your steadfast love come to me, O LORD, Your salvation according to Your promise; then shall I have an answer for him who taunts me, for I trust in Your Word. And take not the word of truth utterly out of my mouth, for my hope is in Your rules. I will keep Your law continually, forever and ever, and I shall walk in a wide place, for I have sought Your precepts. I will also speak of Your testimonies before kings and shall not be put to shame, for I find my delight in Your commandments, which I love. I will lift up my hands toward Your commandments, which I love, and I will meditate on Your statutes.

In this section, the psalmist expresses his unwavering trust in God's Word and teaches us to do the same. Those who trust in the LORD will not be disappointed. The Scriptures say, "Everyone who believes in the Lord will not be put to shame" (Ro. 10:11). God's law is good for us. It frees us from slavery to sin and sets us on the path of freedom to live according to God's will. Delight in God's law brings about conformity to Christ. In His life as well as in His death, Christ sought to do nothing except that which pleased His

Father in heaven (John 4:34). Our salvation is guaranteed and secured by the Lord Jesus Christ who perfectly obeyed the law of God both in His life and in His death. Everyone who adheres to the Word of God and places His trust in Him, will not be disappointed on the last day. Because of Jesus Christ, we too (like the psalmist), can say to the LORD our God, "I trust in Your Word" (v. 42); "I will keep Your law continually" (v. 44), and "Your commandments which I love" (v. 47, 48).

Let Your steadfast love come to me, O LORD,
Your salvation according to Your promise, for Jesus' sake,
Amen!

Comfort in God's Word
(Psalm 119:49-56, *Zayin*)

Remember Your Word to Your servant, in which You have made me hope. This is my comfort in my affliction, that Your promise gives me life. The insolent utterly deride me, but I do not turn away from Your law. When I think of Your rules from of old, I take comfort, O LORD. Hot indignation seizes me because of the wicked, who forsake Your law. Your statutes have been my songs in the house of my sojourning. I remember Your Name in the night, O LORD, and keep Your law. This blessing has fallen to me, that I have kept Your precepts.

The psalmist teaches us three things here. Firstly, God's promises given to us in His Word must be the basis of our prayers. These are the prayers that are guaranteed answers for they are surely according to God's own will. Praying God's Word back to Him, is true praying. It is the kind of praying that truly moves the heart of God. Secondly, the Word of God stirs up within us a hatred for sin. To the righteous, sin is disgusting for it is against our holy, righteous and loving God. Finally, the Word of God gives comfort to

His people in times of affliction. "When I think of Your rules from of old, I take comfort, O LORD" (v. 52). The LORD God will always work for (not against) His people even when He ordains affliction in their lives. When the righteous remember this, they are stirred up in their souls to pray to God and to keep His law delightfully. Christ is the Song of the redeemed for in Him is all the fullness, holiness and love of God shown to His people.

How sweet the Name of Jesus sounds
In a believer's ear!
It soothes his sorrow, heals his wounds,
And drives away his fear.
(John Newton)

The Lord My Portion
(Psalm 119:57-64, *Heth*)

The LORD is my portion; I promise to keep Your words. I entreat Your favor with all my heart; be gracious to me according to Your promise. When I think on my ways, I turn my feet to Your testimonies; I hasten and do not delay to keep Your commandments. Though the cords of the wicked ensnare me, I do not forget Your law. At midnight I rise to praise You, because of Your righteous rules. I am a companion of all who fear You, of those who keep Your precepts. The earth, O LORD, is full of Your steadfast love; teach me Your statutes!

The LORD is precious to the soul of every true believer. Nothing less or other than God can truly satisfy. St. Augustine concurring with this truth said, "You have made us for yourself, O Lord, and our hearts are restless until they rest in You." Thus, the psalmist is not only zealous for God's praise, but He is pleading for divine blessing. He prays with his whole heart for God's blessings promised in His Word because he knows that his life depends on them. Nothing will separate him from God and His Word. He therefore runs to Him and pleads for mercy and God is pleased to grant His request. May we be given that deep longing for the glory and blessing of God in our lives that we will be willing to forsake all for Him. This points us to the Lord Jesus who forsook all in order to seek the glory of God the Father in the salvation of His chosen ones. Like Christ, may we find our ultimate joy in pursuing God and His will regardless of the cost (Heb. 12:2).

As a deer pants for flowing streams, so pants my soul for You, O God.
My soul thirsts for God, for the living God.
When shall I come and appear before God?
Psalm 42:1-2

God Moves in Mysterious Ways
(Psalm 119:65-72, *Teth*)

You have dealt well with Your servant, O LORD, according to Your Word. Teach me good judgment and knowledge, for I believe in Your commandments. Before I was afflicted I went astray, but now I keep Your Word. You are good and do good; teach me Your statutes. The insolent smear me with lies, but with my whole heart I keep Your precepts; their heart is unfeeling like fat, but I delight in Your law. It is good for me that I was afflicted, that I might learn Your statutes. The law of Your mouth is better to me than thousands of gold and silver pieces.

William Cowper's poem entitled, *God Moves in Mysterious Ways,* comes to mind when one considers this section of this great psalm. Cowper's poem, as does this section of Psalm 119, points us to the fact that the LORD God is always working for the good of His people. Regardless of how God may deal with us at times, He treats us better than we actually deserve. Yes, He is always working all things for His glory and for the good of His people (Ro. 8:28). Often, God's people are prone to wander away into sin. As a Good

Father and because of His love, He disciplines His wayward children (Heb. 12:5-11). In such times, we are to praise Him as the psalmist does here, "Before I was afflicted, I went astray, but now I keep Your Word" (v. 67). We need to remind ourselves that "nothing will separate us from the love of God which is in Christ our Lord" (Rom. 8:39).

Judge not the Lord by feeble sense,
But trust Him for His grace;
Behind a frowning providence
He hides a smiling face.
(William Cowper)

Man's Chief End
(Psalm 119:73-80, *Yodh*)

Your hands made and fashioned me; give me understanding that I may learn Your commandments. Those who fear You shall see me and rejoice, because I have hoped in Your Word. I know, O LORD, that Your rules are righteous, and that in faithfulness You have afflicted me. Let Your steadfast love comfort me according to Your promise to Your servant. Let Your mercy come to me, that I may live; for Your law is my delight. Let the insolent be put to shame, because they have wronged me with falsehood; as for me, I will meditate on Your precepts. Let those who fear You turn to me, that they may know Your testimonies. May my heart be blameless in Your statutes, that I may not be put to shame!

The answer to the first question in the *Westminster Shorter Catechism* teaches us that "Man's chief end is to glorify God and enjoy Him forever." This is the purpose for which the LORD God made us. However, since the Fall (Gen. 3), sin has rendered all mankind unfit for this purpose. Left to himself, man is unable to glorify and enjoy God as he should. Yet, in His mercy, the LORD has provided a way for man to be restored to his original state. In Christ, the Second Adam, the LORD God broke the power of sin over man. On the Cross of Calvary, Christ dealt with our sins once and for all. Because of this, all who trust in Him can join the psalmist as he sings to the LORD, "…Your law is my delight" (v. 77). Christ's redemption, frees us to worship and enjoy the Lord with a pure heart.

O Lord, let Your mercy come to me,
That I may live; for Your law is my delight.
Thank you for saving me from my sins.
In Jesus' Name, Amen!

Unwavering Faith in the Word of God
(Psalm 119:81-88, *Kaph*)

My soul longs for Your salvation; I hope in Your Word. My eyes long for Your promise; I ask, "When will You comfort me?" For I have become like a wineskin in the smoke, yet I have not forgotten Your statutes. How long must Your servant endure? When will You judge those who persecute me? The insolent have dug pitfalls for me; they do not live according to Your law. All Your commandments are sure; they persecute me with falsehood; help me! They have almost made an end of me on earth, but I have not forsaken Your precepts. In Your steadfast love give me life, that I may keep the testimonies of Your mouth."

Often in life, our circumstances do not always match what we believe. Sometimes, our struggles with remaining sin, and fear of the unknown future, shake us up and disturb our inner peace. Yet in these situations, it is necessary for us to keep trusting in the LORD and His Word. Every problem that comes in the way of God's children has an expiry date. The Apostle Paul exhorts us not to lose heart, "for this light momentary affliction is preparing for us an eternal weight of glory beyond all comparison" (2 Cor. 4:17). In His Word, God assures us of eternal peace and safety through His Son, Jesus Christ. We ought to take comfort in the fact that He is busy working to perfect His image in us because we are His in Christ Jesus our Saviour.

In Your steadfast love give me life, that I may keep the testimonies of Your mouth, Amen!

God's Word, Unchanging and Unchangeable (Psalm 119:89-96, *Lamed*)

Forever, O LORD, Your Word is firmly fixed in the heavens. Your faithfulness endures to all generations; You have established the earth, and it stands fast. By Your appointment they stand this day, for all things are Your servants. If Your law had not been my delight, I would have perished in my affliction. I will never forget Your precepts, for by them you have given me life. I am Yours; save me, for I have sought Your precepts. The wicked lie in wait to destroy me, but I consider Your testimonies. I have seen a limit to all perfection, but Your commandment is exceedingly broad.

In Act V, Scene V of William Shakespeare's *Macbeth*, we hear Macbeth soliloquizing, "Life's but a walking shadow; a poor player, that struts and frets his hour upon the stage, And then is heard no more; it is a tale told by an idiot, full of sound and fury, signifying nothing." True indeed! Life is passing away. Everything is passing away. Kingdoms come; kingdoms go. However, in this section, the psalmist reflects on God's Word which is "firmly fixed in the heavens" and His faithfulness which "endures to all generations" (vv. 89-

90). Jesus said, "Heaven and earth will pass away, but My words will not pass away" (Mat. 24:35). As children of God, we put no confidence in the flesh nor in the wisdom of this world. Our confidence is in the Word of LORD and in the LORD of the Word! We must build our lives on Jesus Christ, the Incarnate Word. He is our only Sure Foundation. He is "the same yesterday, today and forever" (Heb. 13:5).

You will keep him in perfect peace
Whose heart is steadfast
Because he trusts in You.
(Isaiah 26:3)

God's Word, A Sure Guide
(Psalm 119:97-104, *Mem*)

Oh how I love Your law! It is my meditation all the day. Your commandment makes me wiser than my enemies, for it is ever with me. I have more understanding than all my teachers, for Your testimonies are my meditation. I understand more than the aged, for I keep Your precepts. I hold back my feet from every evil way, in order to keep Your Word. I do not turn aside from Your rules, for You have taught me. How sweet are Your Words to my taste, sweeter than honey to my mouth! Through Your precepts I get understanding; therefore I hate every false way.

God is the Fountain of all true wisdom. He has given us His wisdom in Christ and in His Word. If we are to be wise, we must seek this wisdom in God's Word. As an old preacher once said, "A good man carries his Bible with him, if not in his hands, yet in his head and in his heart." God's Word alone is a trustworthy guide in our daily living. The grace of God enables us to receive His Word and own it. When we are taught and mastered by the Word of God, we become wise unto salvation (2 Tim. 3:15). The Word of

God is greater than the world's greatest teachers because it finds its source in the All-wise and Eternal God. Hence the psalmist can sing, "O how I love Your law! It is my meditation all the day" (v. 97). Meditation on the Word of God gives us divine wisdom. The wisdom of this world is foolishness before God. Christ, who is in us, is "the power of God" (1 Cor. 1:24).

Lord, teach me to love Your law and to meditate on it day and night – for Jesus' sake, Amen!

God's Word, Our Light
(Psalm 119:105-112, *Nun*)

Your Word is a lamp to my feet and a light to my path. I have sworn an oath and confirmed it, to keep Your righteous rules. I am severely afflicted; give me life, O LORD, according to Your Word! Accept my freewill offerings of praise, O LORD, and teach me Your rules. I hold my life in my hand continually, but I do not forget Your law. The wicked have laid a snare for me, but I do not stray from Your precepts. Your testimonies are my heritage forever, for they are the joy of my heart. I incline my heart to perform Your statutes forever, to the end.

We live in such a dark world. It is a world in which it is often difficult to tell right from wrong because there is so much darkness all around. The moral relativists want us to believe in moral subjectivism as they try to press us into their mold. But when we look into the Word of God, we see light. Through His Word, God directs us, step by step, on the path of righteousness for His Own Name's sake. The children of God are children of the light (Eph. 5:8; 1 Thes. 5:5). The children of the light seek to walk in the light. They have a strong desire and longing for holiness. They plead with the LORD for greater grace. They live their lives under the Word of God. Their real comfort comes from the LORD. They hold on to His precepts and promises. The psalmist ends this section by praying for persevering allegiance to the statutes of the LORD; "Incline my heart to perform Your statutes forever, to the end" (v. 112). This is the constant cry of those who have been transferred by God in Christ from the kingdom of darkness into His marvelous Kingdom of light. They desire more and not less of this light to the end. May the LORD grant it to us through Jesus Christ, His Son, our Savior, who is also the Light of the world (John 8:12).

This is the message we have heard from Him and proclaim to you,
That God is light, and in Him is no darkness at all.
If we say we have fellowship with Him while we walk in darkness,
We lie and do not practice the truth.
But if we walk in the light, as He is in the light,
We have fellowship with one another,
And the blood of Jesus His Son cleanses us from all sin.
(1 John 1:5-7)

For at one time you were darkness, but now you are light in the Lord.
Walk as children of the light (Eph. 5:8).

Love of God's Law; Hate of the Wicked
(Psalm 119:113-120, *Samekh*)

I hate the double-minded, but I love Your law. You are my hiding place and my shield; I hope in Your Word. Depart from me, you evildoers, that I may keep the commandments of my God. Uphold me according to Your promise, that I may live, and let me not be put to shame in my hope! Hold me up, that I may be safe and have regard for Your statutes continually! You spurn all who go astray from Your statutes, for their cunning is in vain. All the wicked of the earth you discard like dross, therefore I love Your testimonies. My flesh trembles for fear of You, and I am afraid of Your judgments.

The closer we come to the searching light of God, the more aware we become of the sin within our hearts and the sin around us. The more we become aware of sin, the more we will hate our sin. The more we hate sin, the more we will love the LORD and His Word which keeps us from sin. Sin is disgusting to those whose hearts have been made alive by the saving grace of God in Christ Jesus. Being aware of our tendencies to wander off into darkness, we tightly hold onto God even as He tightly holds onto us. God's saving grace is to the believer, sustaining grace. This grace preserves the believer to the end. While the saints are striving to enter God's eternal rest, they are, at the same time, resting in the merits of their great Saviour, Jesus Christ. One day, all strife shall cease. All wickedness shall be exposed and judged and the children of God will live in eternal bliss with their Savior in the Presence of God.

You are my hiding place and my shield; I do hope in Your Word, Amen!

My Eyes Long for Your Salvation
(Psalm 119:121-128, *Ayin*)

I have done what is just and right; do not leave me to my oppressors. Give Your servant a pledge of good; let not the insolent oppress me. My eyes long for Your salvation and for the fulfillment of Your righteous promise. Deal with Your servant according to Your steadfast love, and teach me Your statutes. I am Your servant; give me understanding, that I may know Your testimonies! It is time for the LORD to act, for Your law has been broken. Therefore I love Your commandments above gold, above fine gold. Therefore I consider all Your precepts to be right; I hate every false way.

The eyes of the righteous are constantly fixed upon the LORD for He alone is their righteousness and salvation. This is the gospel call to all who would be saved, "Turn to me and be saved, all the ends of the earth! For I am God, and there is no other" (Is. 45:22). The psalmist in this section responds to this call by faith. He trusts in the LORD alone for his salvation when he says, "My eyes long for Your salvation and the fulfilment of Your righteous promise" (v. 123). He does not trust in his own righteousness even when he says, "I have done what is just and right…" (v. 121). After we have done all, we must look to the LORD for salvation asking Him to establish the work of our hands through Jesus Christ. Every spiritual blessing we receive comes to us from God through Jesus Christ who gradually works His life in us. Then we begin to adore Him and His Word above all earthly treasures because He becomes more precious to us.

Turn my eyes upon Jesus, LORD.
Help me to look full in His wonderful face.
And as I do so, may the things of this earth fade away,
In the light of His glory and grace
For His Name's sake!
Amen!

The Wonders of Redeeming Love
(Psalm 119:129-136, *Pe*)

Your testimonies are wonderful; therefore my soul keeps them. The unfolding of Your words gives light; it imparts understanding to the simple. I open my mouth and pant, because I long for Your commandments. Turn to me and be gracious to me, as is Your way with those who love Your Name. Keep steady my steps according to Your promise, and let no iniquity get dominion over me. Redeem me from man's oppression, that I may keep Your precepts. Make Your face shine upon Your servant, and teach me Your statutes. My eyes shed streams of tears, because people do not keep Your law.

Towards the end of his life, John Newton, the author of the famous hymn, *Amazing Grace* said, "…Though I am not what I ought to be, nor what I wish to be, nor what I hope to be, I can truly say, I am not what I once was; a slave to sin and Satan…" The Apostle Paul wrote in 1 Cor. 15:10, "…by the grace of God, I am what I am…" Redeeming love is always the theme of the righteous. When we stop to meditate and reflect on the wonders of God's redeeming love, our hearts are lifted to heaven and we enjoy sweet and intimate fellowship with our God and Father through Jesus Christ, His Son and our Saviour. The Scriptures make the vision of heaven clearer to us. We are then brought to experience the joys of heaven and are made aware of the pain of living outside the grace of God. Our hearts are propelled to weep for the salvation of the wicked through the merits of our Lord and Saviour, Jesus Christ who shed many tears on our behalf while He was here on earth.

There is a fountain filled with blood,
Drawn from Immanuel's veins,
And sinners plunged beneath that flood
Lose all their guilty stains.

E'er since by faith I saw the stream
Thy flowing wounds supply
Redeeming love has been my theme,
And shall be till I die.
(William Cowper)

God and His Word, Righteous Altogether
(Psalm 119:137-144, *Tsadhe*)

Righteous are You, O LORD, and right are Your rules. You have appointed Your testimonies in righteousness and in all faithfulness. My zeal consumes me, because my foes forget Your words. Your promise is well tried, and Your servant loves it. I am small and despised, yet I do not forget Your precepts. Your righteousness is righteous forever, and Your law is true. Trouble and anguish have found me out, but Your commandments are my delight. Your testimonies are righteous forever; give me understanding that I may live.

Righteousness is a necessary attribute of God. God cannot be unrighteous. He cannot do wrong and has never done wrong to anyone. God's righteousness extends to everything He does and everything He says. Thus, it is right to say as the psalmist does at the opening of this section, "Righteous are You, O LORD, and right are Your rules" (v. 137). It is fitting to say that about God, not man. God stands by every word He says. Man doesn't. We all know the disappointment caused by unfulfilled promises. We have disappointed other people by breaking the promises we made to them and they have disappointed us the same way. We know the pain of untruthful and hurtful words spoken against us. We have been lied to and we have lied; we have been hurt and we have hurt others – because we couldn't keep our promises to them. But the LORD is different. He is righteous. Therefore, we can always trust that He will fulfil every promise that He has made. When He speaks, He always speaks truth. His Word is truth and is good for us. He is not man and He cannot lie (Nu. 23:19). He is able to do everything that He says He will do (Ro. 4:21). All of God's promises to us are fulfilled in Christ Jesus (2 Cor. 1:20). In His life, death and resurrection, Christ fulfilled all righteousness on behalf of God's people as promised in His Word.

Your testimonies are righteous forever; give me understanding that I may live. Amen!

Answer Me, O LORD!
(Psalm 119:145-152 – *Qoph*)

With my whole heart I cry; answer me, O LORD! I will keep Your statutes. I call to You; save me, that I may observe Your testimonies. I rise before dawn and cry for help; I hope in Your words. My eyes are awake before the watches of the night, that I may meditate on Your promise. Hear my voice according to Your steadfast love; O LORD, according to Your justice give me life. They draw near who persecute me with evil purpose; they are far from Your law. But You are near, O LORD, and all Your commandments are true. Long have I known from Your testimonies that You have founded them forever.

Here in this section, we see a desperate cry of the psalmist to God. He cries to God for salvation and pleads for life. He hopes in God's Word and meditates on it as he waits for an answer from God. He is not bitter against God or resentful towards Him. He trusts that the LORD alone is able to grant his request. This man wrestles with God in prayer. The language of his request certainly borders on blasphemy when he says to God, "Answer me!" It's reminiscent of Gen. 32:26 where Jacob, wrestling with God, says, "I will not let You go until You bless me." Jacob knew, as did the psalmist, that his life depended on God's answer to his prayer. Therefore, in desperate and yet bold faith, he lays hold of God by faith with confidence that his request will surely be granted. The psalmist pleads with God in this way on the basis of His "steadfast love" (v. 149). God knows our needs. He cares. We too, can boldly approach His throne of grace through Jesus Christ (Heb. 4:15).

Before they call, I will answer; while they are yet speaking I will hear (Is. 65:24).

A Sure Redemption
(Psalm 119:153-160 – *Resh*)

Look on my affliction and deliver me, for I do not forget Your law. Plead my cause and redeem me; give me life according to Your promise! Salvation is far from the wicked, for they do not seek Your statutes. Great is Your mercy, O LORD; give me life according to Your rules. Many are my persecutors and my adversaries, but I do not swerve from Your testimonies. I look at the faithless with disgust, because they do not keep Your commands. Consider how I love Your precepts! Give me life according to Your steadfast love. The sum of Your Word is truth, and every one of Your righteous rules endures forever.

Adherence to God's Word naturally works assurance in the lives of His redeemed. The more we hold on to God's Word, the more assured we become of His promises to deliver us from affliction. There is no better weapon with which to build our confidence in God's deliverance in times of need. The psalmist gives us a window into his heart and life. He shows us the source of his confidence. He says, "I do not swerve from Your testimonies" (v. 157). 1 John 2:1 tells us that Christ is our Advocate. He is our Redeemer.

He is the Source of life. Unlike the ungodly, God's children have direct access to God through Jesus Christ. He hears their cries and answers them according to His will. The ungodly have no interest in God or their spiritual wellbeing. They do not care about God, Christ and His Word. On the contrary, those who love God love Him and His Word and strive to walk in obedience to Him by His grace. Christ is their Greatest Interest. They rest in Him, fully assured of their eternal redemption through His cross.

O LORD give me life according to Your steadfast love through Jesus Christ, Amen!

The Beauty of God's Word
(Psalm 119:161-168, *Sin and Shin*)

Princes persecute me without cause, but my heart stands in awe of Your words. I rejoice at Your Word like one who finds great spoil. I hate and abhor falsehood, but I love Your law. Seven times a day I praise You for Your righteous rules. Great peace have those who love Your law; nothing can make them stumble. I hope for Your salvation, O LORD, and I do Your commandments. My soul keeps Your testimonies; I love them exceedingly. I keep Your precepts and testimonies, for all my ways are before You.

The love of God's Word gives the believer the spiritual ability to endure whatever issues life throws at him. Those whose hearts have been captivated by the Word of God are often too caught up by the wonder of God's Word to be bothered about the petty issues of life. Their hearts and minds are lifted up to heaven. They love what they see in God's Word. They see God's truth. They abhor falsehood. The sight of God's truth gives birth to love for Him and His Word in their hearts. In turn, His Word produces great peace in their hearts so much so that "nothing can make them stumble" (v. 165). Psalm 19:7-11 uses very high and exalted language to describe the wonder and beauty of God's Word. God's Word is of precious value to all who will be taught by it. God's Word points us to Christ who purchased eternal peace for us by reconciling us to the Father through His death on the cross (Isa. 53:5). God sees all our steps. Blessed are those who fear Him. Blessed are those whose hearts are captivated by His Word. Blessed are those who practice God's Word in their lives.

Great peace have those who love Your law; nothing can make them stumble, Amen!

One thing have I asked of the LORD, that will I seek after:
That I may dwell in the house of the LORD all the days of my life,
To gaze upon the beauty of the LORD and to inquire in His temple.
Psalm 27:4

Give What You Command
(Psalm 119:169-176 – *Tav*)

Let my cry come before You, O LORD; give me understanding according to Your Word! Let my plea come before You; deliver me according to Your Word. My lips will pour forth praise, for You teach me Your statutes. My tongue will sing of Your Word, for all Your commandments are right. Let Your hand be ready to help me, for I have chosen Your precepts. I long for Your salvation, O LORD, and Your law is my delight. Let my soul live and praise You, and let Your rules help me. I have gone astray like a lost sheep; seek Your servant, for I do not forget Your commandments.

In what seems like an anticlimactic ending to this great psalm, the psalmist offers a humble prayer to the LORD for salvation based on His own Word. This prayer is fueled by the psalmist's great desire and longing for God and His ways. The psalmist wants his prayers heard and his answer given. His prayer is motivated by a deep sense of humility. He does not approach God on the basis of his eloquence or his obedience. He solely stands on the promises of the LORD God Himself. With his feet firmly planted in God's

Word as his foundation, the psalmist pleads to the LORD for deliverance. One preacher put it like this, "We should always make the Word of God the rule of our discourse, so as never to transgress it by sinful speaking, or sinful silence." The saints break the silence and humbly plead for their salvation in Christ on the basis of His Word. Our God is able to save to the utmost those who draw near to Him through Christ who ever lives to make intercession for His people (Heb. 7:25).

"Come to Me, all who labor and are heavy laden,
and I will give you rest…"
Matthew 11:28-30

Printed in Great Britain
by Amazon